SMOOTH JAZZ

TITLE	PAGE	TRACK WITH MELODY CUE	TRACK ACCOMPANIMENT ONLY
Morning Dance	3	1	2
Bali Run	4	3	4
Just the Two of Us	6	5	6
This Masquerade	8	7	8
Silhouette	9	9	10
Harlem Nocturne	10	11	12
Songbird	12	13	14
Breezin'	13	15	16
Tourist in Paradise	14	17	18
She Could Be Mine	16	19	20
We're in this Love Together	18	21	22

ISBN 978-0-634-02770-3

7777 W. BLUEMOUND RD. P.O. BOX 13819 MILWAUKEE, WI 53213

For all works contained herein:
Unauthorized copying, arranging, adapting, recording or public performance is an infringement of copyright.
Infringers are liable under the law.

Visit Hal Leonard Online at
www.halleonard.com

EWI 4000 - Voice 29
EWI 5000 - Voice 09
EWI 4000 - Voice 21 +

MORNING DANCE

CD

1: With melody cue	
2: Accompaniment only	

By JAY BECKENSTEIN

ALTO SAX

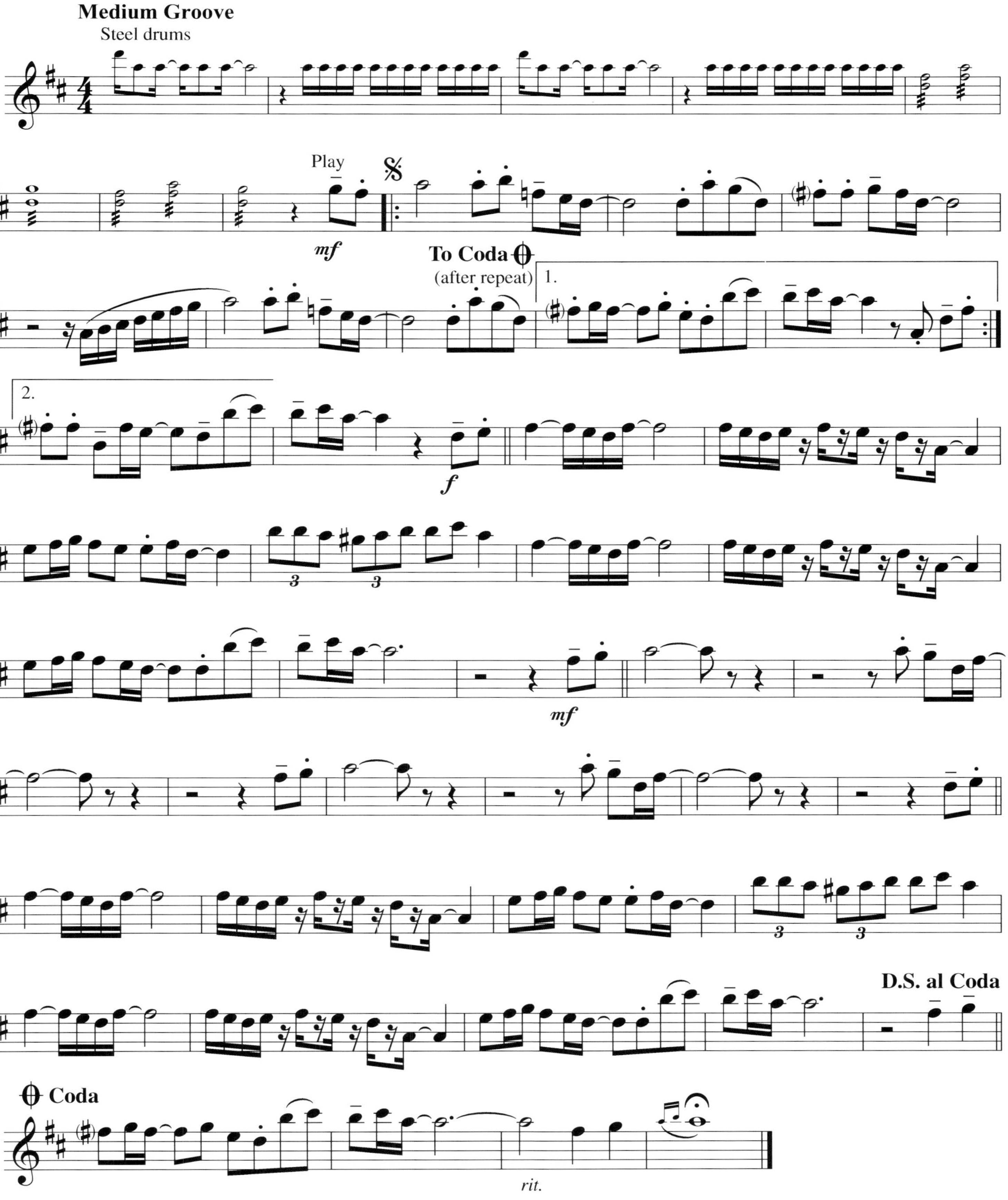

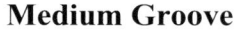

SONGBIRD

CD

13: With melody cue
14: Accompaniment only

By KENNY G

ALTO SAX

Medium (Straight Eighths)

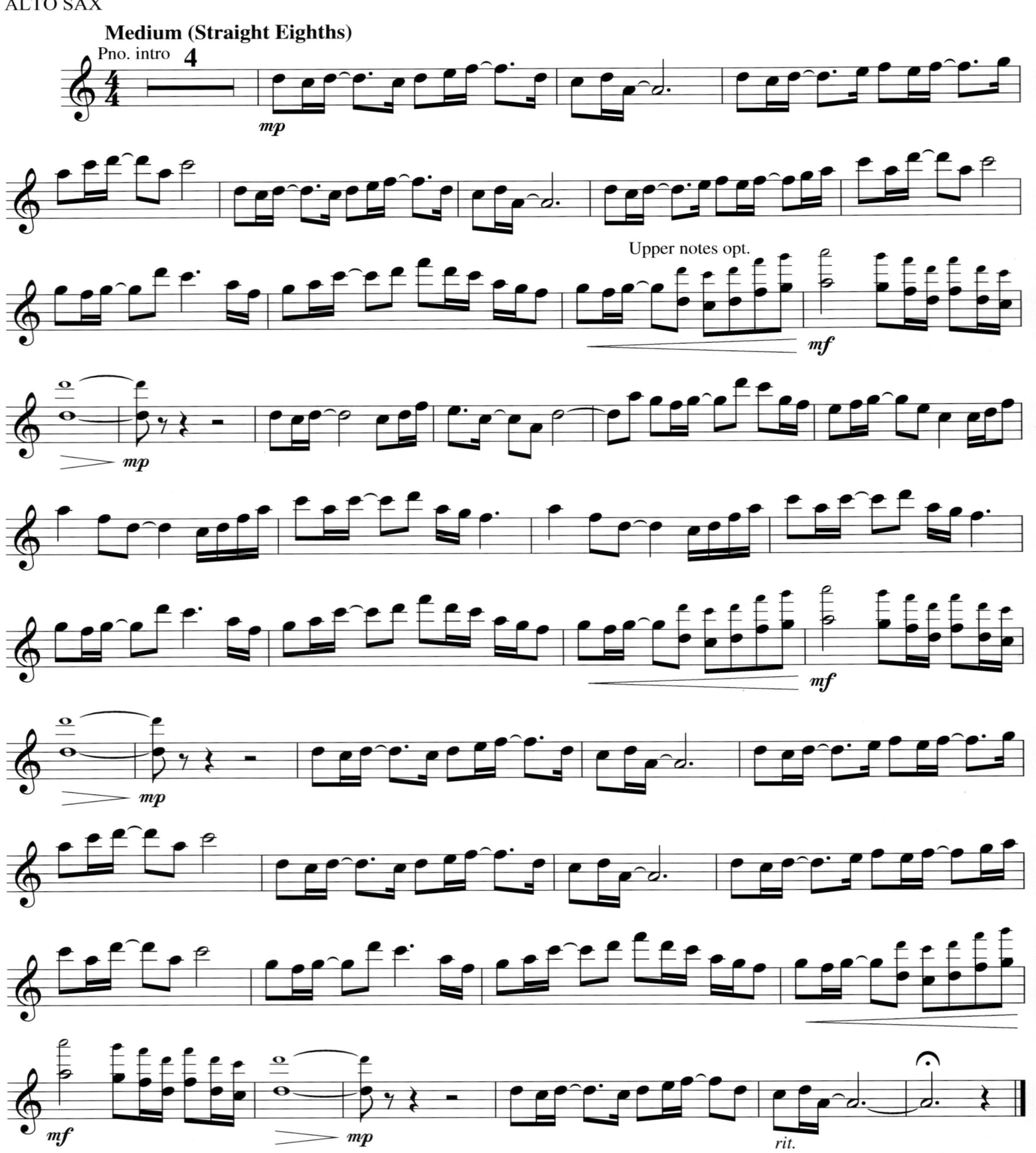

EWI 4000 - Voice 13
EWI 5000 - Voice 73

TOURIST IN PARADISE

CD

17: With melody cue
18: Accompaniment only

By RUSS FREEMAN

ALTO SAX

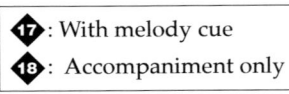

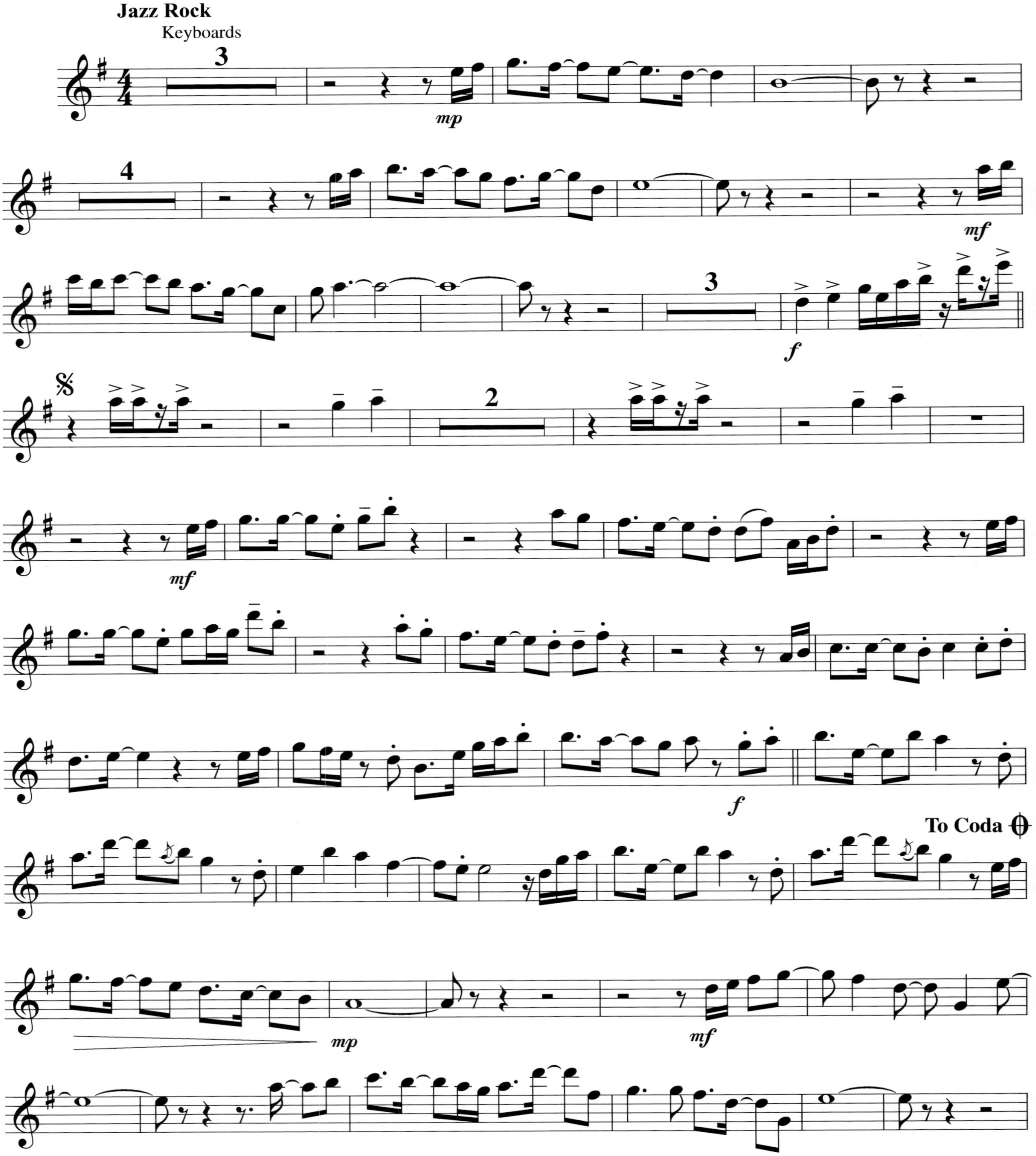

SHE COULD BE MINE

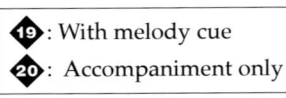

By DON GRUSIN

ALTO SAX

Hal•Leonard Instrumental Play-Along

Your favorite songs are arranged just for solo instrumentalists with this outstanding series. Each book includes great full-accompaniment play-along audio so you can sound just like a pro! Check out www.halleonard.com to see all the titles available.

The Beatles
All You Need Is Love • Blackbird • Day Tripper • Eleanor Rigby • Get Back • Here, There and Everywhere • Hey Jude • I Will • Let It Be • Lucy in the Sky with Diamonds • Ob-La-Di, Ob-La-Da • Penny Lane • Something • Ticket to Ride • Yesterday.
___00225330 Flute................$14.99
___00225331 Clarinet.............$14.99
___00225332 Alto Sax.............$14.99
___00225333 Tenor Sax............$14.99
___00225334 Trumpet..............$14.99
___00225335 Horn.................$14.99
___00225336 Trombone.............$14.99
___00225337 Violin...............$14.99
___00225338 Viola................$14.99
___00225339 Cello................$14.99

Chart Hits
All About That Bass • All of Me • Happy • Radioactive • Roar • Say Something • Shake It Off • A Sky Full of Stars • Someone like You • Stay with Me • Thinking Out Loud • Uptown Funk.
___00146207 Flute................$12.99
___00146208 Clarinet.............$12.99
___00146209 Alto Sax.............$12.99
___00146210 Tenor Sax............$12.99
___00146211 Trumpet..............$12.99
___00146212 Horn.................$12.99
___00146213 Trombone.............$12.99
___00146214 Violin...............$12.99
___00146215 Viola................$12.99
___00146216 Cello................$12.99

Disney Greats
Arabian Nights • Hawaiian Roller Coaster Ride • It's a Small World • Look Through My Eyes • Yo Ho (A Pirate's Life for Me) • and more.
___00841934 Flute................$12.99
___00841935 Clarinet.............$12.99
___00841936 Alto Sax.............$12.99
___00841937 Tenor Sax............$12.95
___00841938 Trumpet..............$12.99
___00841939 Horn.................$12.99
___00841940 Trombone.............$12.99
___00841941 Violin...............$12.99
___00841942 Viola................$12.99
___00841943 Cello................$12.99
___00842078 Oboe.................$12.99

The Greatest Showman
Come Alive • From Now On • The Greatest Show • A Million Dreams • Never Enough • The Other Side • Rewrite the Stars • This Is Me • Tightrope.
___00277389 Flute................$14.99
___00277390 Clarinet.............$14.99
___00277391 Alto Sax.............$14.99
___00277392 Tenor Sax............$14.99
___00277393 Trumpet..............$14.99
___00277394 Horn.................$14.99
___00277395 Trombone.............$14.99
___00277396 Violin...............$14.99
___00277397 Viola................$14.99
___00277398 Cello................$14.99

Movie and TV Music
The Avengers • Doctor Who XI • Downton Abbey • Game of Thrones • Guardians of the Galaxy • Hawaii Five-O • Married Life • Rey's Theme (from *Star Wars: The Force Awakens*) • The X-Files • and more.
___00261807 Flute................$12.99
___00261808 Clarinet.............$12.99
___00261809 Alto Sax.............$12.99
___00261810 Tenor Sax............$12.99
___00261811 Trumpet..............$12.99
___00261812 Horn.................$12.99
___00261813 Trombone.............$12.99
___00261814 Violin...............$12.99
___00261815 Viola................$12.99
___00261816 Cello................$12.99

12 Pop Hits
Believer • Can't Stop the Feeling • Despacito • It Ain't Me • Look What You Made Me Do • Million Reasons • Perfect • Send My Love (To Your New Lover) • Shape of You • Slow Hands • Too Good at Goodbyes • What About Us.
___00261790 Flute................$12.99
___00261791 Clarinet.............$12.99
___00261792 Alto Sax.............$12.99
___00261793 Tenor Sax............$12.99
___00261794 Trumpet..............$12.99
___00261795 Horn.................$12.99
___00261796 Trombone.............$12.99
___00261797 Violin...............$12.99
___00261798 Viola................$12.99
___00261799 Cello................$12.99

Songs from Frozen, Tangled and Enchanted
Do You Want to Build a Snowman? • For the First Time in Forever • Happy Working Song • I See the Light • In Summer • Let It Go • Mother Knows Best • That's How You Know • True Love's First Kiss • When Will My Life Begin • and more.
___00126921 Flute................$14.99
___00126922 Clarinet.............$14.99
___00126923 Alto Sax.............$14.99
___00126924 Tenor Sax............$14.99
___00126925 Trumpet..............$14.99
___00126926 Horn.................$14.99
___00126927 Trombone.............$14.99
___00126928 Violin...............$14.99
___00126929 Viola................$14.99
___00126930 Cello................$14.99

Top Hits
Adventure of a Lifetime • Budapest • Die a Happy Man • Ex's & Oh's • Fight Song • Hello • Let It Go • Love Yourself • One Call Away • Pillowtalk • Stitches • Writing's on the Wall.
___00171073 Flute................$12.99
___00171074 Clarinet.............$12.99
___00171075 Alto Sax.............$12.99
___00171106 Tenor Sax............$12.99
___00171107 Trumpet..............$12.99
___00171108 Horn.................$12.99
___00171109 Trombone.............$12.99
___00171110 Violin...............$12.99
___00171111 Viola................$12.99
___00171112 Cello................$12.99

Wicked
As Long As You're Mine • Dancing Through Life • Defying Gravity • For Good • I'm Not That Girl • Popular • The Wizard and I • and more.
___00842236 Flute................$12.99
___00842237 Clarinet.............$12.99
___00842238 Alto Saxophone.......$12.99
___00842239 Tenor Saxophone......$11.95
___00842240 Trumpet..............$12.99
___00842241 Horn.................$12.99
___00842242 Trombone.............$12.99
___00842243 Violin...............$12.99
___00842244 Viola................$12.99
___00842245 Cello................$12.99

Prices, contents, and availability subject to change without notice.
Disney characters and Artwork ™ & © 2018 Disney

HAL•LEONARD®